Femme Fatale

Miranda Rocha

"Are not flowers the stars of the earth?"

Clara Lucas Balfour

Table of Contents:

 Hurricane

You call me
Woman
As though it were an insult
Perhaps you've forgotten

I am the storm

You never
Saw
Coming

The kind that

Transforms

Sunny blue skies

To pitch black in
Seconds

The kind whose thunder

Shakes the ground
And breaks the sky

Whose rain is not
Small
Shivering
Kisses
But wild and
Rapid waters

I
Am
Not
Small, scattered showers

But a whole
Damn
Hurricane

So the next time
You call me
Woman

Remember
I am not weak

A rain shower
Can be solved
By an umbrella
And erased by the sun

But a hurricane
Becomes
History.

Femme

The day she was born
The Earth
Trembled

The wind whispered to its leaves

Rumors of a girl

Born of fire and lightning

Her veins forged
By the wrath of the sea
Her heartbeat faster than Hermes
With eyes that held

A thousand lives

And cries that shook the sky

The day she was born
The gods trembled.

Honey

Your voice trickles
Like a waterfall
Your smile shimmers
Lips always twitching
With laughter
You glisten
Eyes so deep
I could swim in them

                    You are
                    Seamless

The way your hair sways
Across your back
I could love you

                              Drown me in your sweetness
                                        I beg you

Typhoon

You are
Vicious

Nails on skin

Spark lightning

Bold,

But he likes you blue

Calm and quiet

But they don't call you
A storm
For nothing

Eyes as deep as the
Abyss
Show him how

You walk on water.

Winter

Your pursuit was

Relentless

Green grass covered in
White

Flowers turned to
Glass

Trees shaken of their leaves
You

Demand

To be seen
Frost creeping on windows

They call snow a blanket

But you aren't something
I want covering me

Your love
Is heavy

Like the snow

You laid
On my world

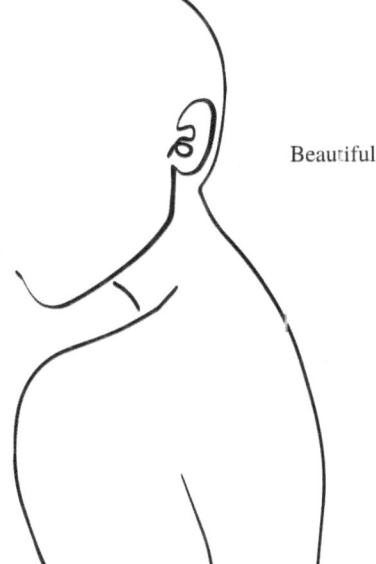

Beautiful,

But damaging
I love you,

But don't touch me

Your snowflakes
Burn my skin

I'm suffocating.

Fire

I will show you passion
Engulf you in these flames
Eyes like blazing embers
I'll remind you why
They remember my name

Earthquake

Call me strong

One
More
Time

While the tremors
Race through me

Just so you
Don't have to
Be there

My faults are rubbing
Against
Each other

Exploding in laughter
Erupting in flames

I am
Unsteady

Seismic Waves

My chaos
Shakes me

But only I
Can save me

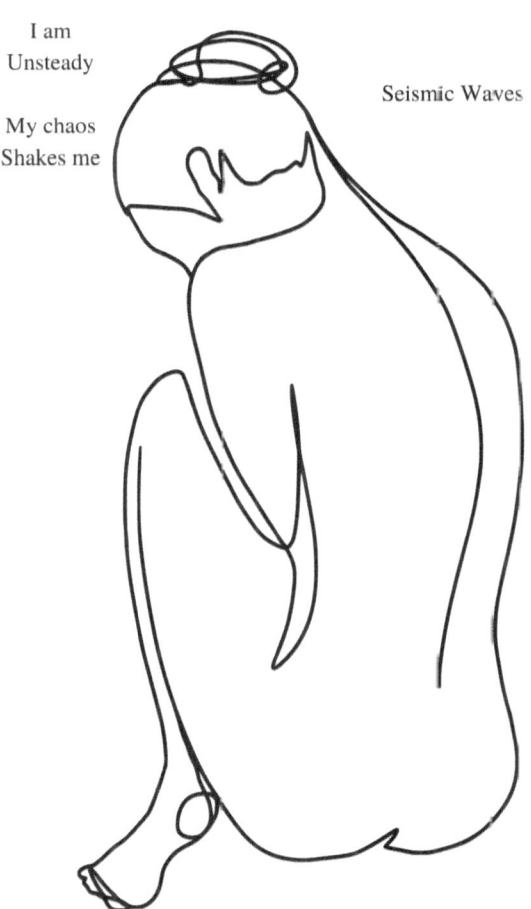

Iridescent

You are kaleidoscope colors

Gleaming through crystal

Shimmering smile, glistening laugh

Shine your light
On me

For even just

A

Moment

Lovely rainbow that you are
Calm the storm within me
Lift my heart
With your
Colors

Show me what it is
To be

Infinite

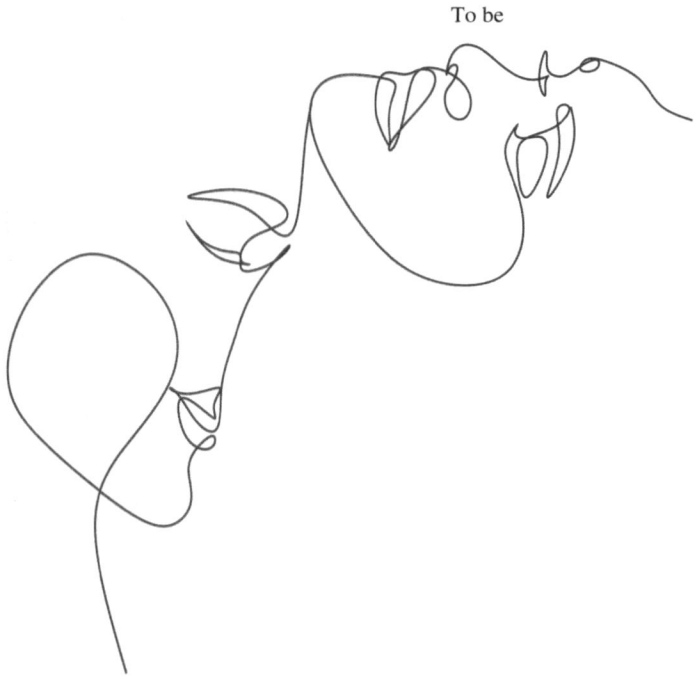

Shimmer

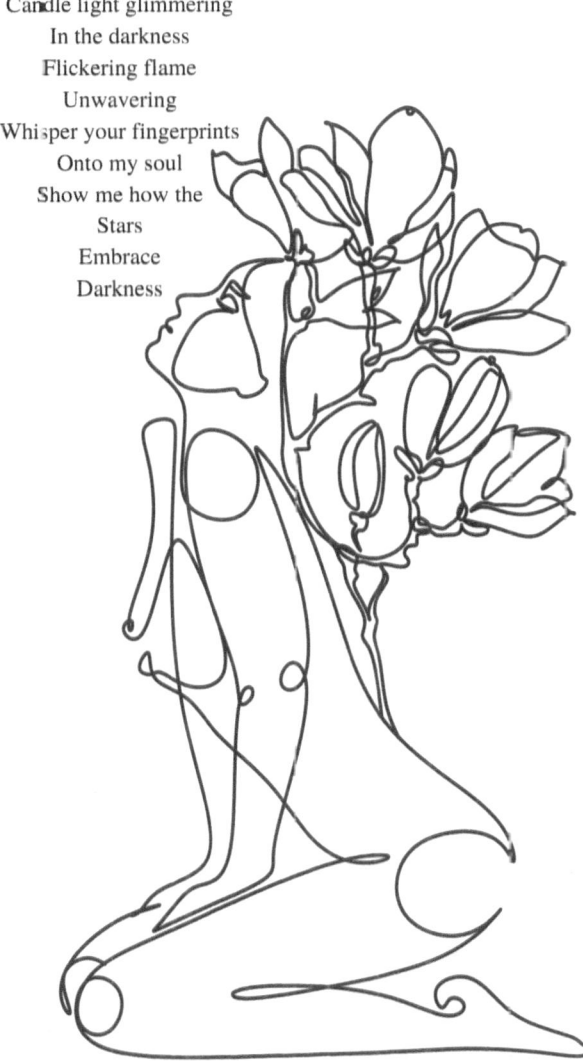

Candle light glimmering
In the darkness
Flickering flame
Unwavering
Whisper your fingerprints
Onto my soul
Show me how the
Stars
Embrace
Darkness

Phases

I will love you
Like a full moon
Loves madness

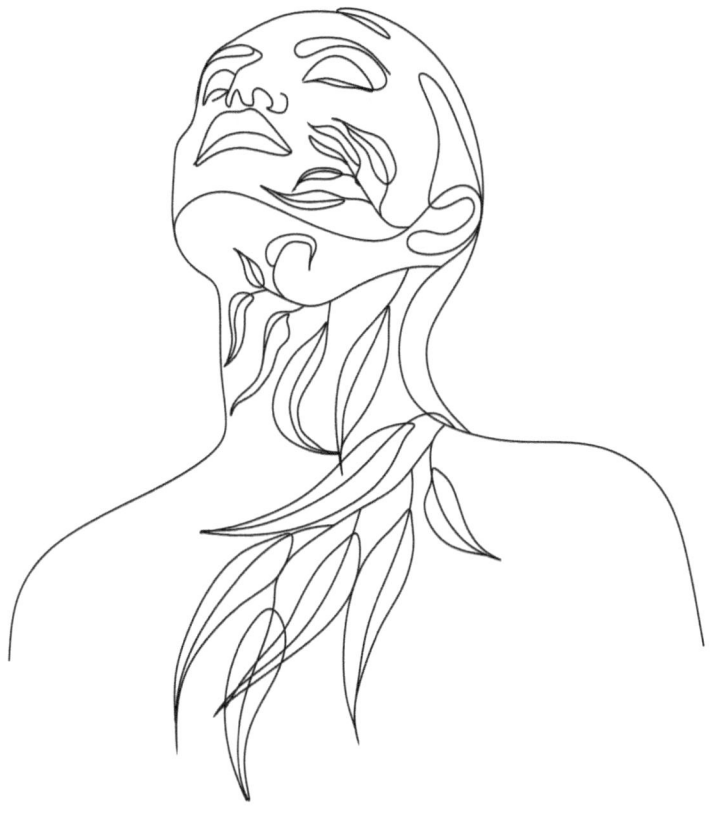

Rose Garden

Whisper your secrets to me

                 Lover

                                 If that's what you wish

                                    To be called,

Holding my stem
So tight

                You bleed

Whisper your

               Sweet nothings

                                          I

                                      Will

                                   Bloom

                                 Anyway

              Through your madness

                 Find your way
           Out of this maze you've built,
                Lover.

Sweetness
Drips from me

Speak of how
These purple petals

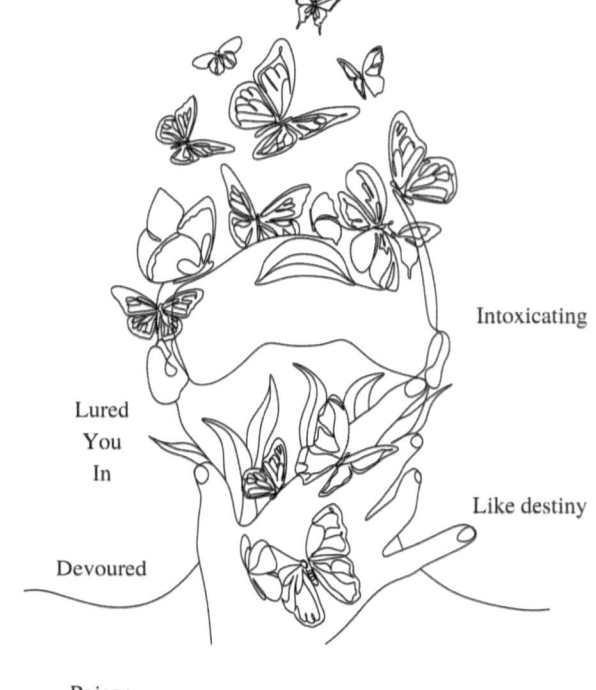

Intoxicating

Lured
You
In

Like destiny

You

Devoured

My scent
Swallowed kisses
Filled with

Poison

You embraced
Your body's

Surrender

While I

Laid you

To rest

Eclipse

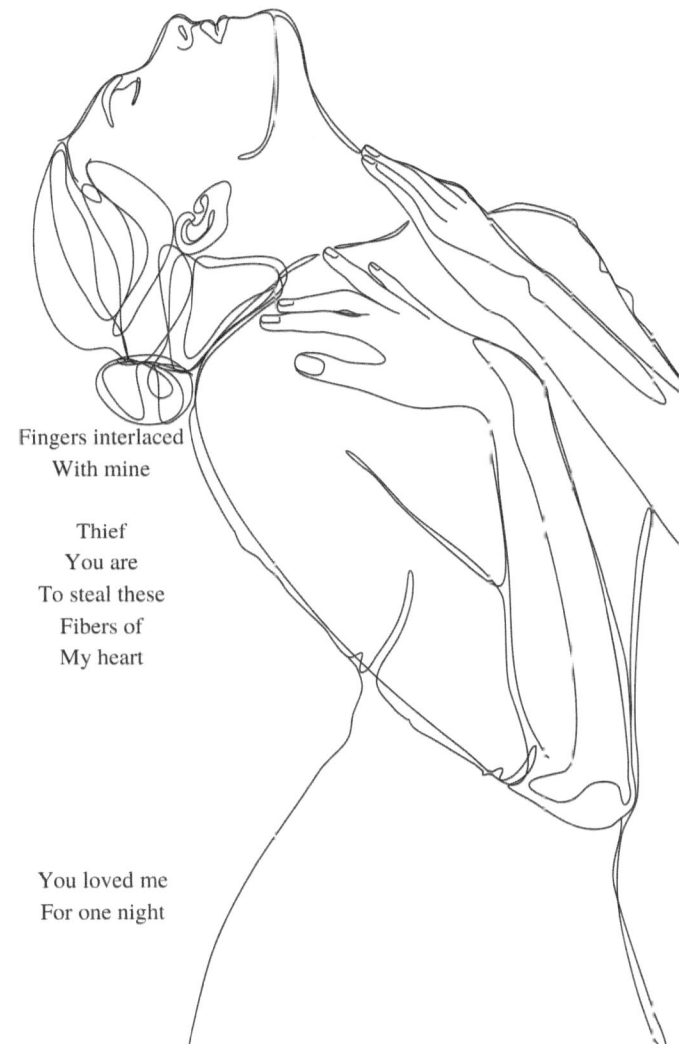

You linger,
A calm
Quiet
Wave

What a gentle

Fingers interlaced
With mine

Thief
You are
To steal these
Fibers of
My heart

While you
Stroked my spine
And explored
These Curves
You've left me with
Unrest

You loved me
For one night

You were gone
Once darkness
Made room for
Light.

Stigmella

You whispered
Sweet little moth
Drawn to my flame
Let me destroy you
Until your skin
Is covered with my name

Kintsugi

Show me your wreckage
We are all damaged souls
You have picked up the pieces
I will fill your cracks with gold
Step into the fire
I'll bring you in from the cold
You only ever looked fragile,
Girl soldered with gold.

Flytrap

I don't want your lips
With all of their
False
Promises
Or you and all of your

I don't want your arms
To Surround Me
With those

You call passion
Don't place your head
On my shoulder
Like my body
Is your rest area

Stop treating me
Like the bed you've made
To lie on

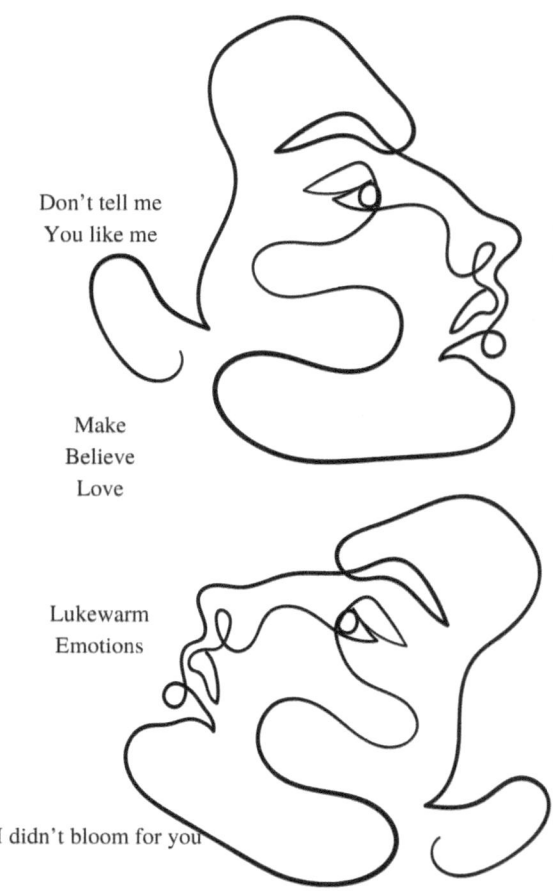

Don't tell me
You like me

Make
Believe
Love

Lukewarm
Emotions

I didn't bloom for you

I am anything
But comfortable

Siren

Let me be your abyss

Look at me
Until your lungs
Burn
Release your gasps

I will drown you

In these waters

I will consume you
Like no other.

Torrent

You were an avalanche
I was summer
You melted at my feet

If there is anything I have in common with the sun
It is that I, too, am burning.

Wildfire

Cover me in hashtags
Call me a trend
Spread me over the internet
Like you spread yourself
Between their legs
Call me a movement
You think I'll fade away
I am just like
Everything on the internet
I will never go away

Weeping Willow

It's been tiring

          Hasn't it?

Your branches

                      Bending
                        Every
                        Wh..ch
                        Way

In the winds
Of storm

           After
           Storm

                      Your leaves
                      Weighed
                      Down

By this

           Rain

These winds
Have
Bent you

                      But they
                      Will
                      Not
                      Break

You
Your roots are
Buried
Deep
In this Earth

                      You will
                      Survive

To see the sun
Bear it's light
On you
Again

Oil Spill

Those hands that
Dance on skin
That voice that
Calls my name
With your pitch black
Depths
I let you in
An ocean
Lit aflame

Tidal Wave

Eye of the storm
Let me stand with you
Calm in your chaos
Like the ocean breeze
With those electric blue eyes
What do you see
Lightning flows with your veins
My darling
Come away with me
If you are the tsunami
Let me be your sea

Hades

In this absence of light
We are everything

Anomaly

I am not
Your salvation
Ever changing waters
Are not meant
To be tamed

Wind

Tell me what I am
If not words
Written on paper
A whispered voice
Yearning to touch you

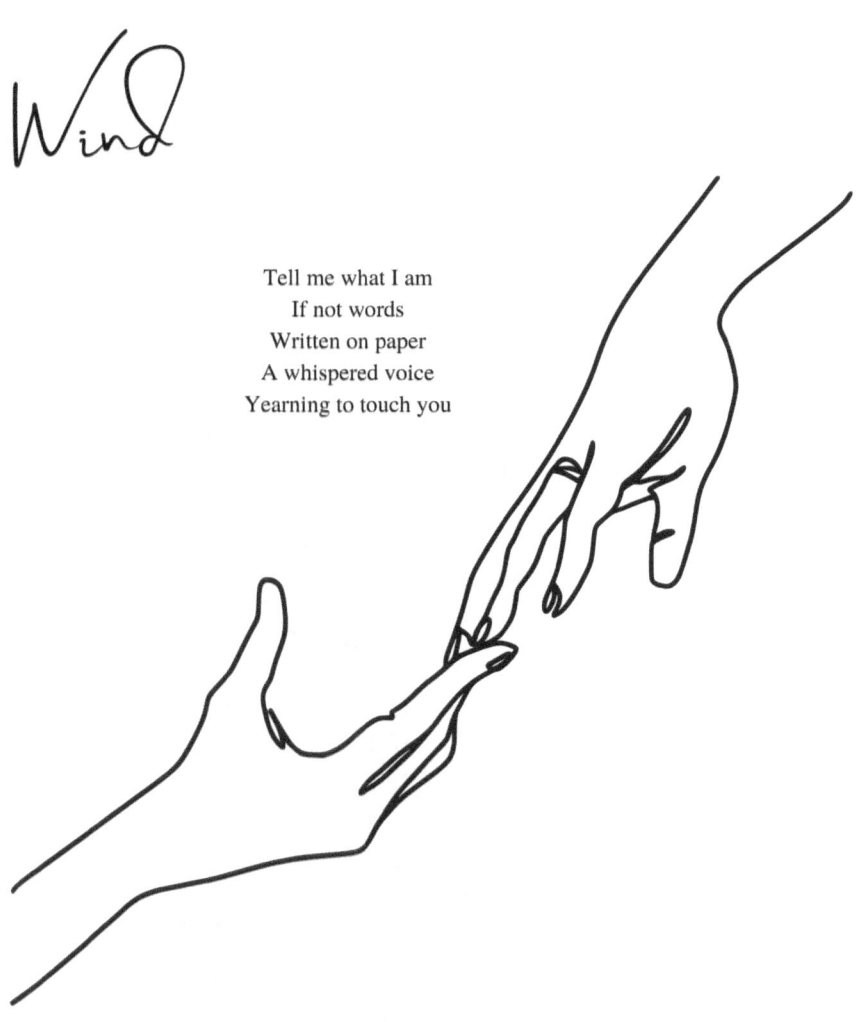

Mountain

You
In all of your
Stillness

You have
Steadied
These footsteps
Before

Haven't you?

A voice
That
Carries
Through the branches

I have
Heard
You

Who are you
If not the

Center
Of my world

My heart trembles
Just to look
At you

If I could have
An Eternity

It still
Wouldn't
Be
Enough

Comet

Shooting Star
Sprinkle your stardust on me
She who makes these galaxies part
Your footsteps shining in the dark
You will lead the way

Diosa

You are gold,
Glistening beauty
And a hint of unrest
Unleash your chaos
You were not meant
To be afraid
Of the monsters
Of men

Her

Chaos wrapped in skin
Unnerving
You make my soul
Quiver
With every step
Beauty must surely be
Jealous
Hands that caress the galaxy
Lips that change destiny
I am a fool for you

About The Author

Miranda Rocha is a CEC, (Chief of Existential Crisis), and a contemplative procrastinator. Based out of South Texas and transplanted to Austin, Rocha spends her time building Lego sets, visiting museums, being an amateur photographer and thinking about what she could be doing - but isn't doing. She is a mother to an eight year old dog named Bear, whom deserves to be named in this publication simply for being the bestest boy, but also for all of the moral support he provides.

www.ingramcontent.com/pod-product-compliance
Lightning Source LLC
Chambersburg PA
CBHW030528130626